SCRIPTING
Your Own Life

How To Create Lasting Change

Tam Veilleux

Scripting Your Own Life © 2014
All rights reserved worldwide.

REVISED 2015

ISBN-13: 978-1495215247
ISBN-10: 1495215245

Inside Out Enterprises
Tam Veilleux
P O Box 116
Freeport ME 04032

No part of this book may be reproduced or shared in any form without the express written consent of the author. That being said, if you're a creative, conscious and cooperative collaborator, contact me at the above address or via email: tam@choosebigchange.com

TAM VEILLEUX
Transformational Coach

Transformational coach and speaker Tam Veilleux is on a personal quest to make creating change easy, fast and fun. As a NLP certified EFT practitioner and member of The Inspirational Women's Leadership Association she enjoys leading workshops while also leading individual clients across the country to create the personal Big Shifts needed for real-life momentum.

A long and deep dive into happiness psychology, neuroscience, the human energy system, personal development, EFT "Tapping", NLP, and hypnosis are just some of the tools Tam. She introduces both ancient healing technologies alongside new mind-hack strategies for training your brain and your mind to work together toward your success.

For a free mini-course in "How To Change Your Mind" and more information on the science, spirituality of change please visit www.ChooseBIGChange.com.

"Nothing changes until you do."

Dedication

To my son, my daughter and my husband – without all of you, I am a black and white film with no sound. Thank you for bringing color and laughter to my life. I recognize that all of you are my creation, my own perfectly scripted movie, and thank you for for being super stars.

Disclaimer

Healing and medicine are two different disciplines and the law requires that you be made aware of this.

My quest is a spiritual one. A portion of my work is holistic energy work and holistic life coaching. I have trained for several years in Emotional Freedom Techniques and energy healing.

The opinions I am about to give do not replace your usual medical treatments or maintenance. In case of serious illness consult your practitioner of choice. This is not diagnosis nor prescription. Any suggestions made in this book are yours to accept or reject.

Do not use any techniques if common sense tells you it is not appropriate.

You must hold harmless the author of the Tapping Scripts book series. Tamra L Veilleux (AKA Tam and/or Tam I Am Veilleux) her assigns or heirs due to her intention to help promote your good health, relaxation and general well being. This is an offer of insight into self-help and self-healing solutions.

Ultimately, your health and wellness is between yourself and God.

Contents

Tam Veilleux: Transformational Coach iii

What To Expect 1

Seeing The Bridge 3

The Invisible Field 5

Control or Be Controlled 7

Thoughts Are Things & Energy Follows Thought 9

The Bubble Gum Brain & Personal Responsibility 13

It's All Just BS 15

Oh, CRAP 19

The *Hit List 21

Personal Pain 23

Yogurt & Personal Responsibility (yes, again) 25

The Brain As The Cam Corder 29

Perception is Projection 33

Pressing Replay 37

Reframing 41

Voice-Overs (Self-Talk) 43

Your Inner Me As The Enemy 47

Becoming An Award Winning Producer 49

A Standing Ovation 51

Resources For Scripting A Life You Love 55

CHAPTER 1
What To Expect

Enlightenment. Managing your outcomes. Energy. Tapping. Synchronicity. Creating your own reality. Neuroscience? The Law of WHAT? Attraction?! I can make my WHAT do WHAT?!

It seems that science and spirit have been having a long and illicit affair resulting in little miracles all over the planet. This book will help you connect the dots and bridge the gap, helping you create a life you love.

If it suddenly has occurred to you that there is an order to the universe and that the randomness is not so random, then you're holding the right book. Wanting to know more about the energy that seems to control your current world is a big leap. That you are taking that leap is a big deal.

Perhaps you're a bit confused because you thought "awakening" meant coming out of a night of deep sleep and now suddenly you are hearing that there is a new meaning to the word awakening – and it might be considered SPIRITUAL. *(Ack!)* All these new-age terms that may not be familiar to you are coming from every yogi on the corner and every picture on your Instagram wall.

It's pervasive, this awakening of humanity, and it's here to stay. You may as well get on board.

This book, *SCRIPTING YOUR OWN LIFE*, bridges the gap between science and spirit. It is a mini-reference guide to answer your questions about controlling and creating your own reality. It will help you better understand how your brain (the muscle), and your mind (the energy), and you (the creator), can and do affect your own life. It can help you go from feeling out of control to being the director of your own block buster, A-list filled, million dollar movie.

This is your little piece of reference material, the kind of information you want to keep in your back pocket for the next time you find yourself hankering for a ham sandwich on the ride home and having one show up on a plate the second you walk through the door. You want to be able to explain these things to yourself before making reservations for a padded room. (By the way, yes, the sandwich thing actually happened to me, and yes, the ham sandwich was as delicious as expected.)

SCRIPTING YOUR OWN LIFE is spoken simply so that all of you who aren't quite awake can sip your coffee and drink in the deliciousness that comes with understanding your personal power.

Welcome to waking up.

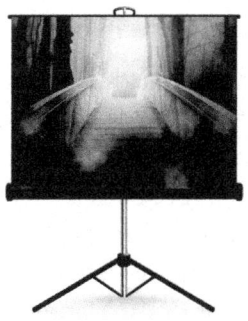

CHAPTER 2
Seeing The Bridge

Some people require hard facts and statistics in order to accept information into their belief system, while other people are naturally willing to allow in knowledge and honor it based on "gut feelings" or an intuitive knowing. These people tend to prefer a softer approach. My goal is to include some of both types of teaching while maintaining a KISS (Keep It Super Simple) method of communication.

Let's start with a basic statement: **Every person has the capacity to be all they can be.** Why? Because energy follows thought. You see – every person already has the tools to support their own transformation. These tools are inherent in each human being regardless of their current exterior life conditions because what we know between science and spirit is that *"energy follows thought."*

Some basic Science: Brain studies have proven that though there are many physical pieces to describe the composition of the muscle that manages us, there are various segments that can be lumped into two basic categories of function, the explicit and the implicit brain. The explicit brain is the area that is demonstrative and can explain through verbal communication, writing and physical action what it believes. It can say "I want to be a millionaire by the time I'm forty" and really mean it. It's also considered the thoughts we are "conscious" of, you know, the thoughts we are aware we are speaking like that last statement, "I want to be a millionaire by the time I'm forty."

The implicit brain is the area that acts as the memory center. It silently absorbs new events and sorts information, affects cellular structure, embeds and imprints patterns to go with similarly themed information which it either recognizes (neural resonance) or doesn't (neural dissonance). The implicit brain/unconscious mind says "I don't have a good history of money management. That statement about being a millionaire just doesn't jibe with what I know about me. Let's discount that statement." Spiritually, the implicit brain is similar to what we call the unconscious mind.

The goal from a scientific viewpoint is to have your implicit brain *in alignment* with your explicit brain or, in other words, your conscious mind in alignment with your unconscious mind.

What you may not know is that you can affect both areas, implicit and explicit/conscious and subconscious mind anytime you choose. You can retrain your brain, and change your mind, whenever you are ready. But, like any task you take on, it takes attention and practice before the new information will "stick".

Going On Gut – A More Spiritual Approach (or is it?)

Regarding that science and spirituality affair: What many people who use their gut feelings to guide them don't realize is that although it feels intuitive and more spiritual to "go with your gut", there are actually more neurons in your digestive track than in your heart. This means that your gut feeling, that internal knowing that you sometimes feel deep inside of your body, is literally translating energetic intelligence to you. Energy transmission is science. Intuitive knowing is more unconscious and spiritual. Gut feelings are, at least in my mind, science and spirit all at once.

#WHODATHUNKIT: There is a mind/body connection that laboratories across the world want us to look at. The invisible web that sends silent messages between twins living in Boston and San Diego is the same web that triggers thoughts of Aunt Sally ten minutes before she calls you. Science and spirit are continually dancing in and around us. Why don't we all join in? Tango, anyone?

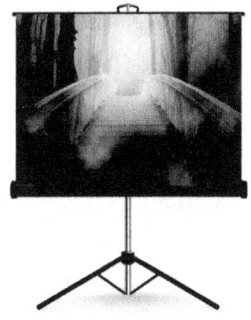

CHAPTER 3
The Invisible Field

The most important piece of the puzzle to your spiritual awakening is that you acknowledge that there is a marriage of science and spirituality. Neuroscientists and quantum physicists have discovered the "invisible web". It's an actual quantum field that connects us. They have admitted to an uber-intelligent energy force that creates inexplicable lab results. Scientists have admitted that they don't know what guides this force. Understanding the invisible web is like trying to catch one of those fluffy dandelion puffs that keeps escaping you every time you swipe at it, every time you think you've got it, you just don't. Quantum Physics is that big and far out of reach, this force that has such a direct affect on our realities.

New information emerges in the field of quantum physics every day. It's best, if we are truly ready to create a new reality, that we simply accept that everything is energy and it travels across an invisible web or grid.

Everything is Energy. Energy Follows Thoughts. Thoughts Are Shaped by Emotion.

Remember from middle school that basic science says that we are made up of cells, atoms, protons, neutrons? Early in the 1900's Thomas Edison and Albert Einstein were the first scientists to report that cells are energy centers, little capacitors that move energy. Cells are everywhere and are every thing. Cells are constantly sending and receiving light vibrations.

Vibrations are energy.

Energy, or vibration, is light shaped by our emotions. This means that each cell (or energy capacitor as mentioned above) is charged energetically by how we feel.

Powerful emotions, both positive and negative, influence the potential of the vibrational waves.

Each feeling you experience, whether positive or negative, is magnetic and affects what you attract into your life. The level of influence that feeling has over you is what determines its level of magnetism. Deep sadness reaps more despair and despondency while joyful enthusiasm gains and attracts to you even more of the same.

#WHODATHUNKIT: As they say in South Africa "Ubuntu", "I am what I am because you are what you are, you and I are one." The invisible web connects and captures our every thought and action and shares it with anyone who is tuned in to the same channel as us. This, in the author's opinion, is reason enough to make your personal movie as beautiful and happy as possible.

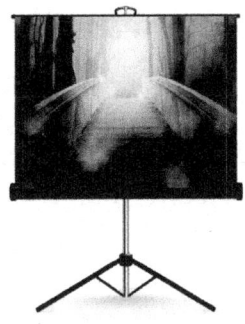

CHAPTER 4
Control or Be Controlled

The basic truth of energy and our emotions is that we affect energy and what it attracts through our emotions. As soon as we learn to control our reactions to life situations, we can control our outcomes.

I have bad news and good news. Bad news first so that you can recover quickly. Chances are high that the old neural patterns that are in force right now in your brain don't really serve your decision making. Current brain patterns and unconscious beliefs control each emotional response. These beliefs began being formed the minute we were conceived. They are based on someone else's perception of the world.

Your parents decisions, your school's rules, the local economy you heard stories about, the church you attended, all of these influences left an imprint in your energy that is affecting you today. In order to change this minute you are in, you must release the energetic imprint of those old memories. Remember: that there is only this minute that you are in. The past is over, the future isn't here yet and there is only right now. Nobody is asking you to pretend your past wasn't real, it's simply time to advance beyond it by making peace with those stories.

It's both a fortunate and unfortunate condition that our cells hold every memory of every thought and feeling we've ever had, even the ones we weren't aware of.

Our cells are way smarter than we know...

...and they are definitely the ones driving the bus of our lives. In order to take control and drive your own bus, you only need to reprogram the energy affecting your cells and help it override the unsupportive, old information.

In order to create a life you love, you must take control of two things:

- Changing the existing emotional patterns in your brain and in your unconscious mind and
- Controlling your emotions around anything that's less than positive to you.

#WHODATHUNKIT: Energy cannot be destroyed – but it can be changed. It is shapeable and formative – you can control it. Nothing about energy is static. Energy remains in constant vibrational motion. Since our cells are always changing we may as well affect what shape they take and how they vibrate by controlling our emotions.

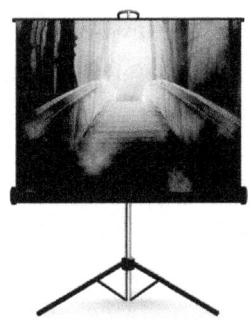

CHAPTER 5
Thoughts Are Things & Energy Follows Thought

From both a scientific and a spiritual point of view, thoughts are things. Laboratories across the world are now measuring thoughts through the use of specialized technology that compute energy waves. We now know that thoughts can and do travel through an invisible field (reread chapter 3 if you've forgotten). Einstein and Edison referred to this grid as the ether. What we speak of here is a invisible web that collects, transmits and receives thought patterns and redistributes them to similarly charged energetic locations. Hence the spiritual term for the law of attraction that says "like attracts like".

Energetic particles rush to meet other energetic particles that have similar vibrational patterns. When enough particles group together (sort of like an energetic flash mob), matter forms. Matter, the stuff the real world is made of, is our reality. And there you go, your thoughts, just became a thing.

In the book *The Secret Life of Plants* by Peter Tompkins we bring it a little closer to home. Mr. Tompkins studied plants reactions to their owners simply "thinking " of returning home to water them. At the instant the plant owner began thinking of watering his plants, the plants reacted positively as though they were anxiously anticipating the water and the love of its human. The plants reacted simultaneously from many miles away. It's one of hundreds of studies that have been made that all prove that energy follows thoughts.

When asked to describe the Law of Attraction many will say "If I think happy thoughts, then good things will happen to me". Though this is accurate, it is also a shallow view of the law of Attraction, because what is also correct is that "what I give attention to grows and expands". If you focus on things that are sad, unhappy or cause distress in your life, you also receive more of that. The law of attraction is not subjective in how it functions, selecting only the high quality thoughts. NO! Whatever it is you give attention to is exactly what you will get more of: good, bad or indifferent. Whether you are doing this consciously or unconsciously is the rest of the story.

You see, even if you are not aware that you are giving attention to something, your brain and mind know and react to it. This makes clearing up the old junk you're storing in your brain more important than ever.

Expansion is the word you want to remember, as is the word "inclusive".

It's true, we live in an inclusive universe.

What you give attention to, even those negative things that you want less of like say "ridiculously long check-out lines", are naturally "included" in your reality.

Are you digging that new Vera Bradley purse, jonesing for better digs and wanting a kinder boss? You'd do best to start giving them a new kind of attention. In David Wilcox's latest book titled *The Synchronicity Key*, he sites major scientific studies that indicate that an energetic channel is formed between yourself and the person or subject you are thinking of. As you think positive or negative thoughts, you either send protons or suck protons from your subject. Protons, the basic structure of light, move at our whims and it happens instantaneously and invisibly. It's best that we consider what we are thinking and where we are aiming! *(Dear Vera Bradley purse, I loooooove your new color, you cool cat, you. Find me soon, won't you?)*

#WHODATHUNKIT: Be careful what you wish for, you're sure to get it.

Tam Veilleux

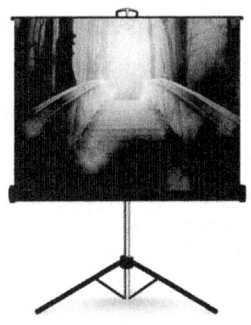

CHAPTER 6
The Bubble Gum Brain & Personal Responsibility

Neuroplasticity is the brain's ability to reorganize itself by forming new neural connections based on behavior changes and environment. How does this translate in layman's terms? For the sake of simplicity, I call it the Bubble Gum Brain.

Imagine taking a wad of bubble gum out of your mouth after you have chewed it for half an hour. Lay it in your hand and look at it. It appears damaged, jagged, torn up. It's a mess...slimy and gross. Now picture this blob as your brain. Pick it up and smooth it. Roll it between your palms or two fingers. Make it into something softer and gentler. Form it however you wish; make it more attractive. The bubble gum can be shaped and formed to be whatever you wish it to be. This visualization explains the pliability of your brain. It represents the scientific term – neuroplasticity. Your brain is like any bubble gum or soft clay, waiting for you to sculpt and shape it.

When you look at neural patterning (cellular patterns) formed by our personal historical reactions to life conditions and learn that these patterns are either in agreement with our wants and needs or out of alignment with them, you can begin to realize that changing the current imprint is imperative to creating change.

And who besides you can make the changes you need? If you said "no one", you're right.

#WHODATHUNKIT: Your brain is able to change at any time. With focused attention and regular practice you can affect its neural patterning for the better. Once you do affect inner change, outer results will come.

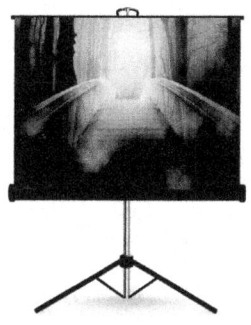

CHAPTER 7
It's All Just BS

Ahem, This is all just BS.

BS or Belief Systems are patterns and habits formed as you witnessed or participated in past events. The reactions you experienced have formed patterns in your brain (science) and in your unconscious mind (spirit) and they now shape your actions and decisions. For example: when you were three your mother may have fed you peas even though you didn't like the taste of them. She made you sit at the dinner table until the peas were all gone. But you were stubborn. You sat at the dinner table staring at the peas and only ate one every half hour until bed time. You fell asleep at your plate quite often. This has helped you decide that:

1. Peas are bad even if you haven't eaten a pea since you were three.

2. Sitting at the dinner table is uncomfortable and torturous and you now prefer to sit with your dinner plate on your lap at the sofa with the television blasting.

3. You prefer going to bed late even though you likely fall asleep on the dinner plate which is on your lap at the sofa and the television is still blasting.

1. You hate hearing what everyone thinks you should be eating.

See how those situations of old may affect you today? Can you see the belief systems that were formed?

It's unfortunate, but we have a natural tendency to pick up the negative rather than the positive.

Belief systems are simply stories we've told ourselves repeatedly that we have not yet challenged. They serve us, or they don't.

Because of the repetition of these stories, your neural system has created patterns in your brain

that honor the story. It received the message so many times that it became part of your internal wiring. Your reaction to the stories is the implicit brain at work. The implied message that "peas are bad" stays with you and affects your current and future decisions, along with your resistance to a delicious meal of crushed peas on poached salmon (yum).

Until we challenge and change the patterns, things will stay the same and change will elude you.

Scientifically, it is the explicit/implicit brain talked about in the previous chapter.

Spiritually, we are talking about the conscious and unconscious mind.

Scientifically and spiritually it's all just BS (belief systems). We may say aloud, "I am going to get a job by Friday" and think we truly mean it. Our conscious mind has made a statement, but our unconscious mind has these memories of you not getting a job interview, or remembers you struggling in between paychecks, or recalls you not wanting to get out of bed in the morning. It replays these old stories that are counter intuitive to you getting a job by Friday. It then sets up roadblocks in the form of situations to deal with to be sure you don't get that job. It's how self-sabotage comes into play.

Self-sabotage occurs when our actions don't align with our desires.

All those proper steps you didn't take, all the excuses you made, and all the newspapers you "forgot" to pick up. They are the reasons you can't move forward into that well paying job.

Your BS overtook your actions and kept you stuck.

When you seem to do everything right, yet no progress is made, what appears to be immobility, is actually your brain actively being directed by the implicit brain/unconscious mind. Your unconscious mind is projecting the perception it holds, which again, is the old belief systems that have been internalized. You have long perceived yourself as unable or unwilling to get work so the brain looks for opportunities to prove you right. The brain is wired so that your occipital lobe (the part that controls your vision) will see the circumstances your implicit brain has predetermined based on your BS (neural patterning).

We are remarkable beings of energy creating our truths based on BS (belief systems) that were formed the minute we took our first breath. Your job now, address those beliefs.

#WHODATHUNKIT: Until you become super diligent in monitoring your inner talk, your BS is making decisions that you may not like.

Tam Veilleux

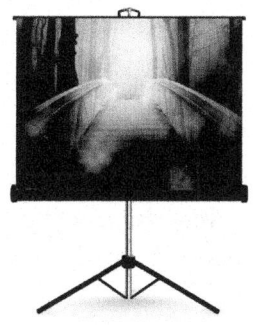

CHAPTER 8
Oh, CRAP

Please excuse my language in this short chapter, but I'm trying to make a point. We can thank John Assaraf and the Praxis Institute for the terrific acronym CRAP which relates directly to your internal BS.

Your brain leans toward negativity and your BS (belief systems) are mostly CRAP.

It's all of your old   **C**onflict

Resistance

Anxiety

Problems.

Whether using spiritual terms like conscious/unconscious mind, or scientific terms like explicit or implicit brain, they both work the same way. Your old habits, patterns, and memories have formed an invisible unconscious way of determining your outcomes. The CRAP is the framework in your unconscious mind and in your brain. It's up to you to uncover the stories and clear the way for new patterns. It's all part of waking up.

What if instead of CRAP you had CAKE in your mind space:

Clarity

Awareness

Kindness

Emotional intelligence

That's much lighter, right? It's time to dig in and do the work.

#WHODATHUNKIT:The CRAP in your brain needs to be attacked with vigor. Leaving the conflict, resistance, anxiety and problems to sit in your brain leaves for a stinking, rotten life.

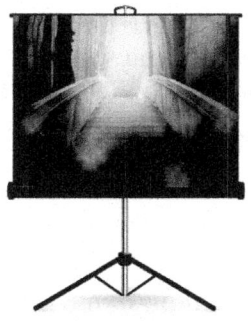

CHAPTER 9
The *Hit List

Before you go forward with change, I encourage you to look back. *No cheating!* Please, do not do yourself the disservice of avoiding your homework. Yes, you are now tasked with creating a personal *Hit List. You are aware now of what your history has done to your brain (science) and your unconscious mind (spirit).

In order to create a life you love, you need to know what needs fixing.

Since we are constantly making decisions and taking actions based on the information we already know…i.e. our history, habits and familiar ways, we can now note them and take action against them. This is you airing your dirty laundry to yourself.

The *Hit List is an inventory of all of your CRAP (conflict, resistance, anxiety and problems). If you change the asterisk before the H into the letter S, you should get the pun. The word you just created when you put an S in front of HIT should help you recognize what gets written down – all the stinky things that have occurred in your lifetime. It's really that simple.

Look back as far as possible to see what has been bugging you. Go to pre-birth conditions. Think back to what you know of your mother's pregnancy. Write down what you know that was negative about her conditions at that time. Since you were inside of her body as a cellular being, shouldn't you assume that you inherently picked up some of those negative thoughts and feelings your mom had, even if you were not aware of them yet? After all, you were intrinsically connected at that time.

Start there, pre-birth, and continue to list the earliest negative memories you can recall. Think of anything you can remember that may not have felt good. Examples are: feeling alone, feeling poor, listening to arguing, being picked on by siblings or others, sexual or emotional abuse, seeing others abuse alcohol or drugs, being left behind, feeling not wanted or unloved. Also list all of the "firsts" that you can remember. First kiss, first day of school, first sexual encounter, first drink, first drug use, first date, first house, first divorce, everything and anything that may have left an impression. Birthday expectations not met. Intentions gone awry. Haircuts that made you feel ugly. List names of those you know you are struggling with today, as well as the reasons you are struggling with them. Name every stinking, sour occurrence you can remember with as many details as you can.

I know that it's a painful process to look at all of these things, but make your list and let it be as long as it needs to be. You don't have to write the details of the condition, just write enough to jog your memory later. If you fill an entire notebook, c'est la vie. Trust that this is useful work to bridging the gap between the life you're in now and the life you want to be in.

#WHODATHUNKIT: You have to know what you're aiming at to begin the work of consciously creating a life you love. The *Hit List means no more living life by default. Since energy follows thought you may as well send it to the right place. This list is the items you need to clear or get neutral on in order to progress.

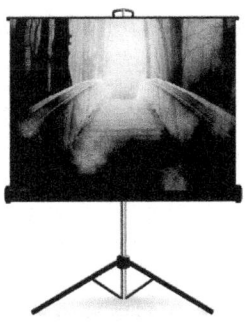

CHAPTER 10
Personal Pain

The root of personal pain is our own perceived identity. But what is your identity and how did you create it?

Your identity is your self-imposed and perceived view of yourself.

I remember my former very vanilla identity well. In my previous life whenever someone introduced me to a new person, I found myself shaking hands and saying "Hi, I'm Tam, I am So and So's mother, So and So's wife, the secretary for the Superintendent, the coach for the basketball team." You could say I felt my identity was "I am no one with out So and So."

What a strange realization it was to wake up and realize that my identity wasn't mine. I was claiming to be everyone else's something or someone. I was the girl-woman with big, blue eyes and a blank stare, saddened by my nothingness. My heart ached, because never was I "a multi-talented artist, an amazing cook and housekeeper, an excellent writer or a woman proud of herself." And never mind loving myself or thinking I was beautiful, those concepts were lost on me. I had no idea who the woman staring back at me in the mirror was, I lost sight of who I was at my core. It took me years of uncovering the complex layers of emotions, events, and memories before I knew the real me. Funny thing, even now, I discover new pieces of me all the time and what do you know, I like who I am. No, actually, I love who I am.

You can (and should) uncover the real you and learn to love yourself, too.

My BS was so broken. For me, it came down to feeling like I didn't deserve more than being "someone's something". Ultimately, it all comes down to your own BS. At some point you have to ask yourself if what you believe is built on what you know, or what you were told. In order to get to your core, that deep place where you hold your own sense of knowing, and discover who you really are, you must eliminate the old beliefs that were formed by other people.

You have to carefully manage what you take in to your brain in every minute and understand that you and you alone are responsible for what goes in and what comes out. Your words and actions need to align with your thoughts. It's important that you get diligent about monitoring yourself in order to lessen and eventually overcome personal pain.

#WHODATHUNKIT:Now is a good time to accept that *Nothing Is Outside of You.* Everything you do, every person you meet, every answer to every question you have is within you. Every result you have gotten is a direct result of your previous thought patterns. You can stop the pain by taking control.

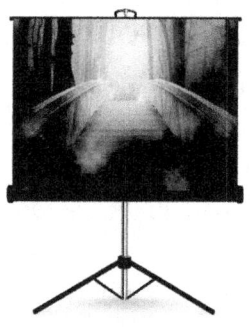

CHAPTER 11
Yogurt & Personal Responsibility (yes, again)

If you believe in a divine source, as I do, then it is possible that you believe that we are all made of the same cosmic stuff. I have said already that everything is energy. There is energy (vibrations and waves) everywhere, including between us (invisible, but there). The energy that is me is also the energy that is you. The energy that is us is also them, and out there, and that desk, and that city and yes, that elephant in Africa.

If we really are one energy, it suddenly becomes extremely important that we shape our lives for bliss. It's like that old saying "If Mama ain't happy, ain't nobody happy." Isn't it true! If you aren't happy and you project negative energy, then somewhere inside of me, even if I am not conscious of it, I am not happy either, because you and I and everyone else are invisibly entwined. Your disgust over Congress's decisions, even if you don't speak it aloud, is affecting everyone as soon as you think it. My frustration with the angry lady in front of me at the post office means two of us were sending out some ugly vibes. *OUCH!* Was that you hurtling anger toward Wall Street?!

Do you still wonder if your thoughts are affecting those people and things that are around you?

Ask the cup of yogurt scientists attached to little paddles. The jiggling blob had an energetic reaction. Once the human being in the other room was told she could have the yogurt and began thinking of eating it, it reacted. The delicious little cup of curd's vibrations changed and measured an energetic reaction on a graph. Technological advances in the last twenty years have made measuring a cup of yogurt a viable way to answer a complicated question about personal responsibility.

Think about it. If our thoughts can affect what seems to be an inanimate object like a carton of yogurt…why would you not suppose that our thoughts affect each and every person around us?

Because we are reflections of each other, it is your personal responsibility to change for the better, and your actions will always speak louder than words. Now that you know how energy moves, take control of every result you produce. Because, friend, you created it in the first place.

Don't pressure yourself. This is not time to panic or feel stressed out that you haven't been "on course". It took you years to form the patterns that are running you, it's going to take some focus to shed your negative BS.

My own trip toward "awakening" continues daily. It started in late 1999, just before the Y2K fiasco. Since then, every few months I experience a new ah-ha moment and a Big Shift toward a better me. You can do the same.

Taking personal responsibility is all about making peace with the past. You'll find with persistence, honesty and constant reflection along with self-evaluation you will create new stories for yourself. These new stories will over-write the old stories that used to run the show.

You came into this world with the ability to choose and were given everything you need to accept or reject your conditions. Some of the most successful people in the world began as homeless, penniless and unloved individuals. Richard Simmons was obese, now he is a slim, trim, fun fitness guru. Donald Trump went bankrupt, rebuilt his business and he's again a multi-millionaire with odd hair. Colonel Sanders of KFC didn't make it as an entrepreneur until he was in his sixties. Abraham Lincoln ran for mayor and failed, congress and failed, the senate and failed. With persistence, he became the man who ended slavery as the 16th president of the United States and he remains one of the most revered men in American history. Did you know Steve Jobs didn't have a college degree? Bill Gates? Mark Zuckerman? Multimillionaires all of them. These people have left legacies and believe it or not, you can, too.

But don't be overwhelmed by my mention of leaving a legacy. You leave a legacy by taking personal responsibility to create the change you need to live your passionate purpose. This simply means you need to make a decision and engage with tools to create change. By the way, Steve Jobs once said he "wanted to leave a ding in the universe." The world is your blackboard and you should leave your mark, too. Take the opportunity to leave your imprint everywhere by being who you authentically are.

Decide today that you want to be remarkable. Your future life and happiness depends on you committing to being the best version of the best vision you have of yourself.

#WHODATHUNKIT: Change is an inside-out job, and it's yours alone to do. You must go inside and make peace with your past so that the new and improved you can live BIG! Choose to take control or else be controlled. Stay stuck or decide to change, it's all up to you.

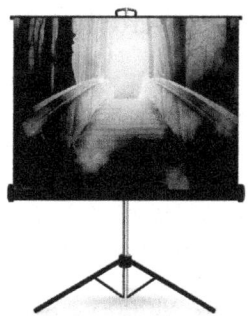

CHAPTER 12
The Brain As The Cam Corder

If you are a typical person with "issues" (*by the way, if you are alive, you have issues*) you probably have caught yourself blaming others for your problems. It's "mother's fault", "daddy's fault", your sister, the aunt, the school teacher, the preacher, the neighbor, the milk man's fault that you are who you are, where you are and what you are right now. It is the ladder's fault that you are afraid of heights, the spider's fault that you are afraid of it, the snake's fault that you fear it, the ocean's fault for being so deep. NO, NO, NO!

First things first. Decide today that there is no "them". There is no single other person or entity that is affecting you. Not the government, the economy, the politicians (well, maybe them), bankers or doctors who have put you where you are. Not your parents or relatives at any level. You determine your life outcomes. Every time, it's only you. Your perceptions, based on your history, create this reality you live.

Let's talk about why this is true.

It will help you to think, from here on out, of your brain as an old fashioned movie projector or a new fangled cam corder. You need to know that you are constantly being shown a film reel of what is going on inside your brain. Your brain is sharing your "perceived" views of stories by projecting them outward through your eyes.

In the spiritual world it's said "the world is your mirror".

You could say it's nearly the same thing scientifically.

Not only is your brain a video camcorder projecting your story, but, like every good movie, there is also a written script. (Don't take this literally, it is only an analogy.)

Think about this. As you experience an emotional event for the first time, you plant a seed in your neural patterns. It's like writing the outline of the movie. Let's use sadness as an emotional event. This movie outline titled "I Am Sad" grows layer after layer of plot and subplots, players and people, locations, smells that support the original idea of sadness. Each page of the script represents the details that are included. The binder for this movie script can be really big or really small. (You are writing this script, so only you know the size.) Each character may have an entire sub script. Each sound may have a simple paragraph or a several pages of descriptive evidence. Each of these items related to the script "I Am Sad" shares a history with you based on how often you bring it to your attention.

For example, you either hated beets or loved them since childhood. The scent of White Musk perfume either brings back a sense of joy and happy family memories or it reminds you of the time your brother dropped an entire bottle of it in the store and then blamed you for it. Men in general may irritate you; women in heels may really send you over the edge. The entire story you tell yourself about any subject is all based on experiences you have had that are stuck in your cellular structure and vibrating outward into reality.

Events that occur, or occurred, leave a neural pattern in your brain. It's an imprint.

The brain will look for information that supports this story you let play in the movie screen in your head. So, if the event you just witnessed matches something that is previously imprinted, the information will find its way there to add to the collection of data. Your brain wants to show you that you are right. It continually looks to support the script it's running.

Some of the stories are happy, beautiful, supportive and loving. Others, not so much. Some of these scripts, the bad ones at a minimum, must be eliminated or neutralized. They take up valuable space in your brain leaving no room for good thoughts and mojo.

Dr. Mark Waldman, one of the world's leading experts on communication, spirituality and neuroscience says it's unfortunate but true that the majority of people are not hardwired for optimism. We gravitate toward negative information. As an easy example think of the national news – why aren't they showing successful rose gardens and local youth sports winners instead of politicians arguing across the aisles? Our history as a species dictated that we use fight, flight or freeze mode when we were club-lugging, spear-throwing cavemen. We were on the lookout constantly because the law of the land was eat or be eaten. Nature wired our brains look for danger. Though we have transformed immensely since our cave-loving days, the backs of the brains still rule the day.

#WHODATHUNKIT: Your current belief systems (BS) are written from the CRAPpy old scripts (old stories of Conflict, Resistance, Anxiety, Problems) in your head. They affect the outcome of your home movies (your current reality). In order to create a block buster movie (read: life), you must rewrite the old script (neural imprints of old events) by changing your perception of what "was" written so those stories no longer play in your home theatre (your brain).

Tam Veilleux

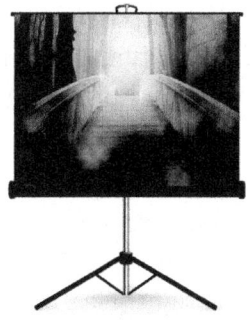

CHAPTER 13
Perception is Projection

What an interesting concept-perception is projection! What this means is how you think you see a situation is how you will project it outwardly. Our past shapes how we see our current experiences. We must neutralize our reactions to the past in order to move forward. If you put one hundred people in an auditorium with only one event going, each viewer will experience the event differently. It depends on where they were standing, what they were focused on and how attentive they were. Each person will see/hear/smell and perceive something slightly different.

If you were one of the one hundred people in the above example then know this: it's more than where you stood, what you focused on or how awake you were. What matters most is your individual history. The situation you watched or were part of was read by your brain based on your BS (Belief System), and the internal already-in-place neural patterning.

Think of your belief system as a filter you would put over your movie camera lens. It colors everything you are taking part in.

Here is an example: If Sally and David are across from Mike watching him eat an apple, as simple as that may seem, they can both end up viewing the scene differently. Let's say Mike bit the bright green apple and winced a bit before chewing and swallowing. Sally may watch this and later report to her friend that "Mike doesn't really seem to enjoy apples. I watched him take a bite and then make a face. Too bad for him; everyone knows that apples are good for you. Mike isn't very smart."

David watched the apple being eaten, too. He remarks to his friend "I watched Mike eating an apple and, lucky dog, he really got a good sour one. I could tell he loved it by the wincing on his face. Everyone loves a sour apple, right? He's just like me! I love a good sour apple. That Mike is one cool cat because he's just like me!"

Two different people, each with their own history of apples and face making, each one with their own very real representation of what happened with Mike. Both viewers made decisions about Mike based on their belief systems and then projected them outwardly by vocalizing what they witnessed. Perception is projection. Their movie camera's filter colored their perception of what they saw.

This kind of thing happens all the time! Both people are right based on their point of view, but at the same time can appear to be wrong based on some other people's point of view. The issue lies in the point of view of the perceiver.

Here is another example. When two men fight, a father and son, they both believe they are right. The father, from his perception is the elder, and is naturally wiser; he deserves respect and Goddammit, if the son isn't going to give him the respect he deserves then he'll smack it into his son. After all, that's how his father before him did it.

The son, from his perception, feels his father has not earned his respect, he's been a bully for too long. He's tired of being hit and screamed at. This time, after he's been hit by his father, he hits back. The father believes he was right, and yet the son feels justified in his own actions. All the while, the mother is in a deep sadness as she reflects on the conflict present in her family. Perception is projection every time.

Think back to arguments you experienced with others. Can you see now how your perception colored your thought process. Can you also recognize how the defendant against you allowed their own perceptions to taint their view? You both were right to look through your own filter.

This is why it's sometimes okay to agree to disagree. Agreeing to disagree makes the most sense, because the defendant's position is based on his perception, his filter, which is formed by his own personal history which you have had no influence over until this moment in time. The same is true of yourself. Your history affects every decision and reaction you ever had. Let it go and move on. You don't have to win over everyone; you simply have to be comfortable with your own BS.

If your BS still stinks, it's time to clean the filter.

If it doesn't – then welcome to waking up.

#WHODATHUNKIT: Every human reality, be it exceptional and abundant or lousy-lucked and full of disdain, is nothing more than a projection of what is going on in the brain and unconscious mind based on their historical influences. Perception is projection.

Tam Veilleux

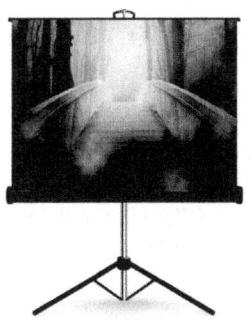

CHAPTER 14
Pressing Replay

Story telling. We all love to do it. Some of us much more than others. Do you know anyone who talks a lot, or more specifically, complains a lot? This kind of person is one who wants their script to be the biggest. They want Hollywood to take on their story. They love their drama so much that they keep pressing replay and blah, blah, blahhing it all in your ear.

This, dear friend, is a major NO-NO if you want a better life. If you are reading this because you are committed to creating change, then stop talking about the old one. Part of your awakening is learning to control what flows into your brain as well as what comes out of your mouth.

Neurologically, what happens every time you retell a story is you imprint the gloom, painful emotion and negative energy into your cells. Remember from earlier chapters, everything is energy and thoughts are measurable things. Retelling your sob story adds heavyweight paper to the script, it makes the print of the story bolder and grows the size of the font you were using. It makes that story take up more space in your cellular structure and helps that story become part of your identity.

The old adage "if you don't have anything good to say, then don't say anything at all" has substance.

Since your ultimate goal is to eliminate every page in the old script of your story that isn't working to your benefit, why add pages to it? The script already sucks. The plot is a mess, why keep retelling it? Just stop talking.

And how, you ask, do I stop talking? You just do. Figure out how to monitor it. Learn to manage it. Find your verbal filter.

When someone asks you "How the heck are you? I heard you were in quite a mess last week." Do something you are not used to: walk away or make light of it. If walking away from the person in front of you isn't an option (and it typically isn't) then you just take the edge off the story and say "Yeah, it wasn't so bad. Anyway, I'm over it now."

Let the story be done. If the person with you persists in dragging the details out of you, stand your ground and say "I don't really want to talk about it. I'm trying to let it go." You'll find the more you do this, the softer the story becomes because the truth is that our memory manipulates memories anyway.

Did you know that your memory slips regularly. The details we thought we captured are not exactly as it happened. Each time we retell the story we move things slightly, exaggerate moments and highlight certain aspects of the story, thereby manipulating it and changing the original memory. It's never exactly the same story two times in a row, especially verbally. Our brains naturally delete, distort and generalize incoming information which means how it happened isn't actually how it happened, there is some level of distortion going on.

The key in discharging negative events is "don't press replay". Do NOT retell your sob stories in full detail. Decide today to tell your stories in *less than ten words*. The longer it takes you to spit out the details of the event, the more of a chance energy has to form a neural pathway in your brain which builds the BS you've been do desperately trying to ditch. Don't let it happen. Control the urge to press replay.

#WHODATHUNKIT: Your brain loves the sounds of your own voice and is hanging on your every word. You'd better make your words serve a better purpose.

Tam Veilleux

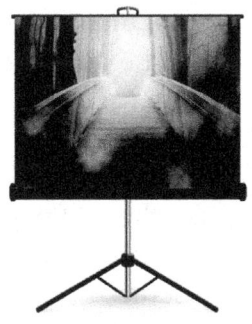

CHAPTER 15
Reframing

If you still must discuss your story, reframe it. Give it a twist!

The meaning of any event depends on how we set it up. When we change the frame of how we look at an event, we change the meaning, and with it – our responses and behaviors. For instance, if someone goes to a party dressed as a skeleton, the meaning is different depending on whether it is Halloween or a funeral. My response to someone slipping on a banana skin is different as an observer than as a victim.

We make meaning from the first impressions we receive. Ultimately, there is always more to the story than what is going on at first glance.

There was an photograph a few years ago of a child's face. He was beautiful, middle-eastern child with gorgeous brown eyes. The eyes of the babe pulled you in and made you care – instantly. When the image expanded to show him full-body it was of four other beautiful children, all of them holding AK-47's. The caption was *"There is always more behind the headline."* The same is true about every event.

Dad and brother may have just duked it out weekly in hours long fist fights. Glasses were broken, bruises formed, each in their hungover fogs, while you stood in the corner cowering. That memory is part of your storyline now. The next best step is to soften the blow and shorten the script. "Dad and Bob had a fight. It got ugly. I didn't like it." Short and concise with not a lot of drama. Now you reframe it. "Dad and Bob are working out their differences. It may have been the last time. I didn't like it, but I don't like seafood, either." With the second sentence you have distanced yourself from the pain, made it smaller.

Some reframing techniques:

Lighten up the drama by softening the edges of the story: (see above)

Turn the problem into a question: (How can Bob and Dad stop getting physical like that?)

Give gratitude for what is right in the situation: (Wow, I'm so grateful that it was over quickly, and now they can both move on.)

Find the positive: (They are figuring out how to communicate in new ways.)

Look at it from a different point of view: (Mom says Dad has been frustrated lately with Bob and maybe he had reached a boiling point.)

Choose to find ways to look at your problems in a new way. It will take the edge off until you can fully discharge the energy of it with deeper psychological tools, like EFT (tapping) [more on tapping later], that permanently change your brain patterns.

#WHODATHUNKIT: By looking at old situations through a new lens and rethinking or reexamining it from a new point of view, you can release the painful emotional charge attached to the memory.

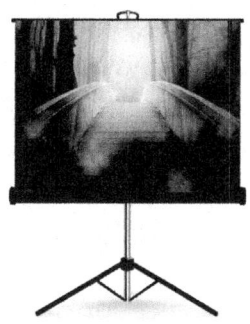

CHAPTER 16
Voice-Overs (Self-Talk)

Become familiar with the voice in your head. You do have one. Check out how it is treating you these days. It may be telling you you are too slow, too fast, too thin, too fat, too messy, too uptight, too, too, too anything and everything. Worse than that is that booming voice-over telling you that you are not smart enough, tall enough, witty enough, financially sound enough, spiritual enough. It's the voice saying that the world is against you and that there are no opportunities available. Poor, poor pitiful you.

Just so you know, that inner voice is simply delivering to you the energy of the script in your head. It's reporting the BS (belief system) and CRAP (Conflict, Resistance, Anxiety, Problems) built into your neural patterning.

Short story about belief systems and self talk. I am not a big girl, never have been. At 5'7" and 125 pounds I was a pretty skinny athlete. I have been keenly aware of my size my entire life because people openly sneer at thin women. But I have never been one to let my size stop me. I loved women's fast-pitch softball and played for many years as an adult. I was in my late twenties and it was the playoffs. We were pitted against our rival team and were losing 9-3 in the top of the fifth inning. It seemed pretty hopeless. With one inning left we needed to make up six runs. Yeah, right.

There was one out when the girl in front of me in the line up got on base. "Good for Ida, she's always doing her job. Now I'll do mine," I said to myself as I lugged my bat out to the plate.

Having the bases loaded didn't really faze me. There was no particular pressure. I was not a power hitter, I batted #1 or #2 in the lineup because I could be counted on to get on base. My penchant for getting base hits made me the Dustin Pedroia of our team. (That's a little Boston Red Sox reference for my New England readers). My plan was to do what I always do- just get on first base and drive in a couple of runs. I had been doing it consistently for many years for this team, this would be no different.

But it wasn't meant to be.

Hitch my pants. Tug my sleeve. Grin at the pitcher. I was set. Two pitches in I pulled back and nailed the ball in a line shot eight or ten feet high that went like a rocket between left and center field. With my sights set on first base I fired up my cleats and took off, hoping the left fielder would trip over her too long sweatpants.

As I got to first base, the coach was waving me on. I glanced at her face which was nearly purple with excitement as her arm wound round and round like a windmill in a tornado. "Go... gooo...goooooo! It's OVER THE FENCE, TAM!!"

Between left and center field...Right. Over. The. Fence. Grand slam. I looked up in time to see the ball roll into an adjacent field. Holy. Cow.

You have never – in your entire life – seen someone wearing gray sweatpants sprint around the bases laughing as hard as I did. I was squealing and jumping and sprinting all at once and I was grinning ear to ear as I crossed home plate after hitting my first-ever home run.

I had never before done that. I didn't know that I could. My arms were skinny. My body was lean. My legs were like long white q-tips. Impossible. But I did it.

A week later I made the newspapers with that terrible photo of me running toward home plate in my sweatpants and crazy smile. I looked drunk. It was not pretty, but I was proud as a peacock.

Regardless of my impossible grand slam, we lost that game and landed in the loser's bracket where in each game thereafter I hit home run after home run. Yes, right over the fence in every game. I had unlocked the BS that kept me from thinking it was a possibility for me to hit a home run. Now, every time I came up to bat everyone was backing up ten or fifteen feet, especially the outfielders! Not only did *they* expect me to nail the ball, I had the same expectation. My internal voice-over was now supporting my life as a home run hitter. It had all boiled down to my BS.

My huge over-the-top enthusiasm during the grand slam event had reprogrammed the cellular structure of my brain and rewired me for power hitting. The coach moved me back in the line up to bat third or fourth position, because now my team supported a new role as a home run hitter. Wow. Me? The toothpick on wheels? Go figure.

Even writing this story brings happy tears to me. Pass the Kleenex.

Your internal chatter matters. It's fate slapping your bottom saying "you can do this, Slugger" or it's saying "Fagettaboudit, Loser." Train your voice to only speak kindness to you and use the delete button on yourself when the voice misbehaves. It'll get tired of your canceling it out and soon you'll only hear the good things. Soon you'll hit your own grand slam in life.

#WHODATHUNKIT: Let the voice in your head speak less of your troubles and more of your dreams and wishes. Mention the magic you witness and do it with enthusiasm. Shush the nay-sayer and welcome a kinder, softer voice.

Tam Veilleux

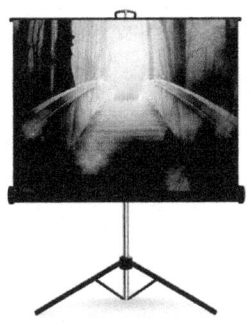

CHAPTER 17
Your Inner Me As The Enemy

Bob is a peer. He works in a nearby city helping people suffering with addiction create lasting change. I met him at a difficult time in my own life as I was dealing with my son's own addiction. Every time Bob and I talk, he tells me he's just an "old Polish guy". He completely identifies himself as that. It's who he believes he is. You know who I think Bob is? I see him as a compassionate retired Navy officer turned addiction counselor with three MBA's who is successful and exudes intelligence. Bob is a person dedicated to making a difference for others. What's lacking is his positive self-identity.

For years prior to discovering who "I" really am, my "who am I" was answered as: wife, mother, aunt, day care provider, volunteer at school, secretary, and a creative person. I was a wanna be Martha Stewart disguised as Mother Goose.

My "inner me" kept me as "wife, mother, aunt" until I realized the real answer to the question of "who am I" was "I am a teacher, healer and artist and I am passionate about making a difference in the world."

Our childhood stories, those old scripts running the show, are filled with with one-liners and beliefs that our family and friends said to us or about us while we were still in ear shot.

Those stories are not real, nor are they true.

You need to pay attention to the Inner Me inside your head. It already has an opinion of you, and it may not be that flattering. You have to decide if this is someone you want to hang out with or not. Never let your Inner Me be your Enemy. Your inner me should be a guiding force of love, joy, silliness, fun, pleasure, and all out bliss. Anything less is unacceptable. Train that voice to speak gently as you wend your way to the top of a well scripted life.

When you hear the inner critic say "You're not good enough" or "Too bad you stink at math," tell that voice to go way. Take a hike. Be gone with its bad self.

Don't let your inner me be your enemy, your inner me needs to be your best cheerleader. Rah. Rah. Rah.

#WHODATHUNKIT: There is much more to you than that voice knows. Now go out and prove it to yourself.

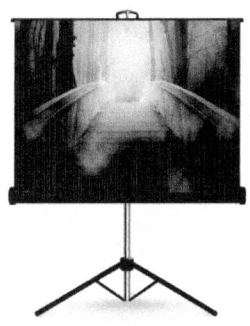

CHAPTER 18
Becoming An Award Winning Producer

By now you're ready for a new reality, you're ready to write a new script!

You know incredible information about your brain (neuroscience) and astonishing facts about spirit (the subconscious). We could go much deeper into the various functions of brain parts and how cells and matter works. Both subjects are much more complex than I have written of here. I will leave the deeper explanations to the quantum physicists and neurologists. On the other hand, we could languish on about spiritual law, karma, cycles, or religion, too, but just understanding at a basic level is all you need to start going from a life lived, to a life loved. Plenty of non-neuroscientists live magnificently charged lives filled with passion and purpose and *control*. That's what this is about – getting control over your mind and your emotional reactions and writing an award winning script for the movie of your life.

> **Your brain captures your every move in high definition.**

Your every word, sight, sound, taste, thought, command, or lament is indelibly imprinted into your cellular structure – permanently. Your old script stays with you, but when you take steps to overwrite it, change happens. This is being fully awake, living out loud with passion and purpose.

Start now to filter everything through the question: *does this incoming data or my reaction toward it serve me?*

Remember that each experience is imprinted into your cellular structure the moment is happens, so just ask that question: *does this serve me?* If the answer is no, then reframe and redirect yourself immediately to begin diffusing whatever it is you have already taken in. The sooner you start canceling out the negative things in your life, the brighter your day will become. It's all been covered in this book. Reread it to be sure your understand all of it.

Energy follows thought and it's all under your control: perfect health, amazing wealth, a deep sense of spirituality and connectedness, excellent relationships, a rewarding career, college degree, second home in Belize, a razor sharp wit or crazy-good dance moves are yours for the taking – when you take control. If my ideas of an amazing existence aren't your ideas of life, that's fine. What matters is that you decide how you want your life to be and then make it happen by taking control of your thoughts.

When you are ready to dig deep and use stronger, more powerful tools – reach out. There are books, coaches, groups and technologies that can help you go from a life lived to a life loved.

#WHODATHUNKIT: Imagine yourself as the mega-star of an award winning script. See yourself living the life of your dreams. You're totally worth it. Contact me today for help in producing an Oscar winning reality.

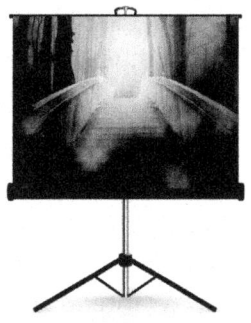

CHAPTER 19
A Standing Ovation

Science is supporting and reporting the results that indicate that indeed, everything is energy that can be directed and reshaped. Choose to self-direct the energetic body that you are, or be affected by outside influences of your energy.

> "With faith the size of a mustard seed, mountains will move."

At least that's what it says in the Bible. Intention drives results. If you want to heal, if you trust the process, you will move your personal mountains. You will divide and conquer, invoking amazing results for yourself. And don't be surprised when the people you interact with suddenly seem to shift, too.

Your own energetic changes will shift your perception of others. It will seem as though they have changed when really, it is only your perception that has changed.

Begin controlling your reality on small surface pains, i.e. your frustration in the long, slow grocery store line, a minor headache, an angry neighbor or co-worker. Track your results by keeping a notebook. As you create successes, write them down. Like any muscle you use, starting slow builds confidence and eases you into the bigger stuff such as finding a new career, or building a new and meaningful relationship. Eventually, you will find yourself working on much larger issues with ease and grace and without worry that it won't work.

Remember always – intention drives results, as does expectations. If your desire is to create a shift in perception, in pain level, in dialogue, then your faith and attention to those matters will create the outcome you hoped for. *Your intention requires your attention.* Your expected result arrives, so always intend the best.

The sooner you attack a problem the better, and you now have no reason to let something fester. Allowing your problem to boil over only makes it bigger, remember to tap into a technique for change as soon as you recognize yourself slipping into a place of negativity. Disrupt your current pattern by saying aloud, "CANCEL, CANCEL!". Squelch it as early as you can so that it doesn't grow into something ugly. Do you need reminders of what your avoidance to problems does? If so, reread this entire book.

Everybody needs tools to create change. You already own the most powerful tool – it's your mind. Supplement its potential with your personal ability to "choose", and then add in EFT tapping and other mind-hack techniques. For additional information about Tapping and it's amazing ability to help you make peace with your past go to: www.choosebigchange.com

Know this: Nothing changes until you do. Until you decide to step into your own personal development and start the process of interrupting old thoughts and installing new empowering ones, nothing will shift.

The ABC's of creating change involve

    A- align with a vision for your new you

    B-address the old BS (belief systems) that hold you back

    C-commit to a set of strategies that will shift you into change

Trust me when I say you are meant for more. We all are. Living up to your true potential means ditching the old stories and writing new ones. It's about writing and living from a script that screams love, happiness, community, perfect health and amazing wealth. You can have all of that and more if you'll only get started.

Create the change you love today. I can't wait to see what kind of script you'll write.

#WHODATHUNKIT: Get support. Decide today to take full responsibility for the script that is running your life. Make peace with your past and creating a new reality.

Tam Veilleux

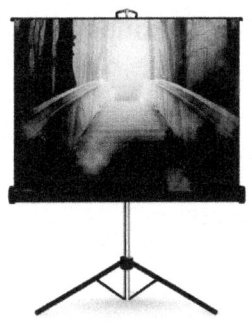

CHAPTER 20
Resources For Scripting A Life You Love

For more information about the ABC's of Change please go to:

www.ChooseBIGChange.com sign up for the free mini-course "How to Change Your Mind". A couple of times a month I'll send you tips and ideas for creating big change in your life.

THINGS TO GOOGLE:

- Neuroplasticity – the brain's ability to be trained
- The Law of Attraction
- Quantum Physics
- Benefits of hypnosis (www.trappersherwood.com and www.wendi.com)
- Learn how to use your brain to affect your happiness level from Neal Slade with his book "Tickle Your Amygdala"

- Benefits of (EFT) Emotional Freedom Techniques (aka Tapping)
- Robert Smith, FasterEFT.com (look at his YouTube videos for free tapping training)
- Access Consciousness

Things To Do

- Write down your goals. Only 3% of people use this simple trick to remind their unconscious minds of what they're shooting for.
- Sticky notes, get some and use them. Post single word reminders or whole sentences of what you are focused on for the week: "breathe deep", "reframe", or "I love you."
- Cut magazine pictures, paste a picture of yourself into them for visual reference to your near future. Keep them nearby to train your brain how you want your future to look.
- Hire a life coach. People who are held accountable are more successful.
- Surround yourself with supportive people. Be sure you have friends and family who are at a place in life where you want to be, too.
- Get a notebook and write your dreams and aspirations in it! Make notes of the wonderful things that happen to you during each day. Your hand writing fires off millions of neurons, use them to your advantage. Read your dream book daily.
- Make a list of supporting beliefs or things that you WANT to believe.
- Search YouTube various TED or TEDx talks. You will find talks on happiness psychology, neuroscience, the law of attraction,

power of prayer, power of meditation and other things that interest you. What you give your attention to expands so focus on happiness

- Do a YouTube search for Tony Robbins, Abraham-Hicks, Jack Canfield, Brene Brown, John Assaraf, Brian Tracey, Deepak Chopra or Kid President

Do The Emotional Detox:
21 Days to a Happier, Healthier, Wealthier You.

www.choosebigchange.com/emotional-detox

Rid yourself of the negative emotions that keep you in a holding pattern of sad, stuck and stressed and develop a higher emotional way of being.

Tam Veilleux

RECOMMENDED READING

"Molly Kite's Big Dream" for kids 7-107 by Tam Veilleux (read the book, see if you can connect the dots between the story and the information you learned)

"Creating Change: Keys to Every Day Alchemy" by Tam Veilleux (at Amazon.com)

"Conversations With God" by Neale Donald Walsh

"Measuring the Immeasurable" an anthology written by various scientists (for those of you who need the science.)

E Squared by Pam Grout (Experiments to get you playing with your own energy powers.)

"The Secret" by Rhonda Byrne (The movie and book that started it all.)

"Ask And It Is Given" by Abraham Hicks

"The Secret Life of Plants" by Tomkins and Bird (more science) The Hidden Messages in Water" Masuro Emoto (If You love Science.)

"Think And Grow Rich" by Napoleon Hill (A classic book for starting your journey.)

"The Biology of Belief" by Bruce Lipton (Best reference if you love science.)

"How God Changes Your Brain" by Andrew Newberg

"The Happiness Code" by Dr Laundre

"Madly Chasing Peace" by Dina Proctor (for the power of meditation in 3 minutes a day)

"What If Up" by Mindy Audlin (for learning how to reframe problems)

The show isn't over.
Welcome to a new beginning.

Remember: "Nothing in your life changes until you do."

Transformational Coach Tam Veilleux invites you to reach out.

email: tam@chooseBigchange.com

Facebook: www.facebook.com/ChooseBigChange

Instagram: @tamrav

Twitter: @thetamiam

Tam Veilleux

ALSO BY THIS AUTHOR

Turn your little readers into little leaders.

The beautifully illustrated children's book "Molly Kite's Big Dream" does everything a children's book should do! With instantly likeable characters, vivid, and entertaining illustrations this is a story that kids will go to repeatedly and there is good news for parents: *Molly Kite stories gently teach important lessons.*

Molly Kite's Big Dream ignites the power of attracting results. The colorful pictures and simple storyline includes basic Law of Attraction steps for conscious caregivers and their little ones. The message of dream, do, have is woven throughout the plot.

As an added bonus the publisher has included conversation starter questions to keep your child engaged in dreaming and taking action.

Available at Amazon.com, CreateSpace.com and MollyKite.com

Made in the USA
Middletown, DE
02 January 2023

21025853R00046